How To Write Online

For Money

Guide To Create And Monetize A Blog For Beginners

Copyright © 2021

All rights reserved.

DEDICATION

The author and publisher have provided this e-book to you for your personal use only. You may not make this e-book publicly available in any way. Copyright infringement is against the law. If you believe the copy of this e-book you are reading infringes on the author's copyright, please notify the publisher at: https://us.macmillan.com/piracy

Contents

What Is A Blog? 1

10 Reasons You Should Start a Blog 2

How to Start a Blog in 6 Steps? 7
    Step 1: Pick A Blog Name 7
    Step 2: Get Your Blog Online 10
    Step 3: Customize Your Blog 12
    Step 4: How to Write A Blog Post & Publish It 14
    Step 5: Promote Your Blog 16
    Step 6: Make Money Blogging 16

How to Promote Your Blog for Free? 17
    How to Promote Your Blog on Other Sites? 17
    Where to Post Blogs for More Traffic? 18
    How to Get People to Read Your Blog More Often? 20
    How to Get Your Blog Noticed on Social Media? 24
    Blog Promotion Using Other Media 29
    How to Get Traffic to Your Blog via Collaboration? 33
    How to Get Blog Traffic via Search Engines? 36
    How to Promote A Blog Using Content Marketing? 39
    Promote Your Blog Using Other Peoples Content 42
    How to Advertise Your Blog? 44
    Promote Your Blog Using Freebies and Competitions 45
    How to Promote Your Blog Using Your Products? 47
    Other Ways to Get Free Blog Traffic 49

How to Make Money with Your Blog? 70
    1. Monetize with CPC or CPM Ads 70

2. Sell Private Ads 71
3. Include Affiliate Links in Your Content 72
4. Sell Digital Products 73
5. Use It As A Content Marketing Tool for Your Business 73
6. Sell Memberships 75
7. Use It to Build Your Credibility 75

What Is A Blog?

In short, a blog is a type of website that focuses mainly on written content, also known as blog posts. In popular culture we most often hear about news blogs or celebrity blog sites, but as you'll see in this guide, you can start a successful blog on just about any topic imaginable.

Bloggers often write from a personal perspective that allows them to connect directly with their readers. In addition, most blogs also have a "comments" section where readers can correspond with the blogger. Interacting with your readers in the comments section helps to further the connection between the blogger and the reader.

This direct connection to the reader is one of the main benefits of starting a blog. This connection allows you to interact and share ideas with other like-minded people. It also allows you to build trust with your readers. Having the trust and loyalty of your readers also opens up the door to making money from your blog, which is something I discuss later in this guide.

10 Reasons You Should Start a Blog

1. You'll Gain Confidence

Blogging is the shy person's stage. You can be center of attention, meeting new people by gaining follows and likes, all within the safety of your own limits. Your blog is your own, whatever you want it to be, and it's a great way of gaining confidence whether it's in the field you're writing in or personal expression.

2. It's A Form of Diary

Writing a diary is long outdated. However, blogging is essentially a collection of diary entries for the world to see. Your blog can be your own secret place on the Internet; anonymous or not, there's a comfort in the thoughts and helpful advice of Internet friends. There are no expectations with blogging, despite the majority of followers being strangers,

3. Blogging Is Great Writing Experience

Trying to get into freelance writing? Blogging is the best way to show your writing is current, and you're writing regularly. As soon as you've created your first post, you're officially published on the Internet, and can promote yourself to companies far more easily by linking your blog than showing outdated articles.

4. There Is Potential Financial Gain

With blogging becoming more and more prolific, there is no doubt that its becoming a profession to be taken very seriously. Blogging is easily a full-time job, if a blog is expected to reach its full potential, and money can be made with hard work and perseverance. Advertising on your blog can help you financially, as can accepting sponsors if you're reviewing products, but ultimately your blog can lead you to a career in blogging, which may seem far off for someone starting a blog, but it's becoming far more acceptable in this day and age.

5. The Blogging Community Is Great

All fellow bloggers want is for other bloggers to be part of the community, and be involved by following blogs and leaving comments. With websites like "Bloglovin" it's easy to have a contained place on the Internet for your favorite blogs, while gaining inspiration for your own posts and articles.

6. It Allows Potential for Self Growth

Broadcasting yourself online allows time for reflection, perspective. You will be able to look back on past work and ideas and learn from them, promoting not only a form of diary entry, but also the idea of self growth. By envisaging your ideas in a public form, it allows your creativity to grow, as well as your confidence and ambitions.

7. It Allows Development of Technological Skills

It is very difficult not to learn basic technological skills while blogging. Whether it's simply editing pictures and using templates, or changing the aesthetics of your blog by using basic coding, you'll learn a lot of basic yet valuable information about the technological age in which we live. Social media, SEO writing, picture formatting—these are all basic skills you can pick up within the first couple of weeks of starting your blog.

8. It Gives People A Creative Outlet

Blogging allows a creative outlet for those who have become consumed by everyday life. By giving you the flexibility to blog when you wish, it can become a way to channel creativity without imposing on your day-to-day responsibilities. What better a way to be creative than in the comfort of your own home, when you have the time to enjoy it.

9. Blogging Is The Current Way to Market A Business

These days, companies are crazy not to have embraced the blogging world. It's all very well having a professional website, but if you use a blog that is regularly updated to show current offers and promotions, clients will see you as more approachable, current, and most importantly more involved in your business.

10. It Creates Opportunities

The final and perhaps most important reason to start a blog: it creates endless opportunities for its owner, whether it be in the form of friendship, financial gain or self-growth, blogging certainly puts your personality out there to the world and gets you noticed in a very unique way.

So what are you waiting for? Go out there and create your own little space on the Internet—you won't regret it.

To be successful as a blogger there is really just one requirement: a passion for your topic.

At its heart, blogging is about sharing your knowledge with the world. Choosing a topic that you are passionate about makes the process of starting a successful blog so much easier. Writing about more than one topic is totally fine too. As long as you are writing about things that you are genuinely interested in, your passion will shine through and keep your readers interested.

So why would you go to the trouble of blogging? There are a few reasons:

- Make money from home. Blogging can be quite lucrative if done correctly. The top bloggers in the world obviously earn quite a bit, but even a part-time blogger can expect to make a nice profit if things are done correctly. The best part about it is that blogging is a form of passive income, since you can spend just a few hours a week writing a blog post and then continue

to make money from it long after the blog post is written. I go into much more detail on how to blog for money later in this guide.
- Share your story. A blog allows you to have a voice and be heard. You can share your story with the entire world if you so choose. One of the most common ways blogs are used are as a diary where the blogger writes about their daily experiences so that friends, family, and others can all be a part of their lives.
- Recognition for yourself or your business. No, you probably won't have paparazzi following you around because of your latest blog post. But a successful blog makes your idea into a reality, and can gain you a ton of recognition in your respective field. Many bloggers are known as experts just because of their blogs, and some have even gotten book and movie deals based on their blogs.
- Find a community. Blogging at its heart is interactive. You write a blog post and people comment on it. This is a great way to connect with people who are interested in the same things as you are. Blogging allows you to teach these people based on your experience, and it gives you the opportunity to learn from your readers as well.

The good news is that the internet is exploding with growth right now. More people than ever are online. This explosion in growth means more potential readers for your blog. In short, if you are thinking about starting a blog then there is no better time than right now.

How to Start a Blog in 6 Steps?

Learn how to create a blog in about 20 minutes following these steps:

1. Pick a blog name. Choose something descriptive.
2. Get your blog online. Register your blog and get hosting.
3. Customize your blog. Choose a free template and tweak it.
4. Write & publish your first post. The fun part!
5. Promote your blog. Get more people to read your blog.
6. Make money blogging. Choose from several options to monetize your blog.

Let's start your blog!

Step 1: Pick A Blog Name
The first step to finding a good blog name is choosing your topic.

If you're not sure what to blog about, there are a few ways to find a good blog topic:

- Hobbies & passions. Hobbies or other interests you are passionate about are a great place to start. Cooking, travel, fashion, sports, and cars are all classic examples. But even blogs about more obscure hobbies can be successful, since the your audience is literally anyone in the world with the internet.
- Life experiences. Everyone has lessons they have learned through life experience. Sharing this knowledge can be incredibly helpful to others in similar situations. For example, I

recently helped a woman start her blog about being a fireman's wife. She has a lot of experience and knowledge to share with others about this topic, and it has helped her connect with others in similar situations. Think about the things you have experienced in life. This could be related to your family (example: a blog about being a stay at home mom), work (a blog about experiences dealing with clients), or other life experiences (a blog about dealing with a troubling time such as a disease or divorce, or about a happy time such as preparing for a wedding or a birth of a child).

- A personal blog. A personal blog is a blog all about you. This will include a variety of topics, from things you do on a daily basis, to random thoughts and musings. This is a great way to share you thoughts with the world without having to stick to just one topic.

Once you have a topic it's time to choose your blog name.

A good blog name should be descriptive so that potential readers can instantly tell what your blog is about just from the name.

If you are blogging about one specific topic then you will definitely want to include that in some way in your blog name. Try not to get hung-up on just one word though. For example, a cooking blog doesn't necessarily have to have the word "cooking" in it. The words "food", "recipes", and "meals" would also let people know that your blog is about cooking.

If you are planning to create a personal blog where you discuss a variety of topics then I recommend using your name, or some variation of it, since your blog is all about you. For example, I own the blog scottchow.com. You can also add your middle name or middle initial if you find your name is already taken. Or you could use a variation like "Scott Chow Blog" or "Blogging with Scott".

Once you have some blog name ideas you will need to choose a domain extension. A .com domain extension is the most preferred, but .net or .org work as well. It is also important to note that for the purposes of a blog domain you cannot have any spaces between words. So "Blogging with Scott" becomes bloggingwithscott.com

Now that you've got your name and have picked an extension it's time to make sure that no one else has already registered the same name

Note: You cannot use any spaces or punctuation other than dashes in a domain name.

If you find that the name you wanted is already taken there are a few things you can do:

- Try a different domain extension. If the .com version is already registered you may still be able to get the .net or .org version of your blog name.
- Add small words. Words like "a", "my", or "the". For example, this site is called TheBlogStarter.com instead of BlogStarter.com.
- Add dashes between words. For example, scott-chow.com

Step 2: Get Your Blog Online

Now that you've got a name picked out it's time to get your blog online. This might sound hard or technical, but the steps below will walk you right through and make the process easy.

To get your blog up and running you need two things: blog hosting and blogging software. The good news is that these typically come packaged together.

A blog host is a company that stores all of the files for your blog and delivers them to the user when they type in your blog name. You must have a blog host in order to have a blog.

You also need to have the software to build your blog. In this guide I will be showing you how to build a blog using the WordPress blogging software, because it is the most popular, customizable, and easiest to use.

The blog host I recommend, and the one I show you how to use in this guide, is BlueHost. I personally use BlueHost and I recommend them for all new bloggers because:

- They will register your blog name for you for free, making sure no one else can take it.
- They offer a free, simple installation of the WordPress blogging software (which I show you how to use in this guide).

- They have been recommended by WordPress since 2005 and currently host over 2 million blogs and websites.
- They have helpful 24/7 customer service via phone or web chat.
- They have a 60 day money-back guarantee if you are unsatisfied for any reason.

1. **Click "get started now".**

2. **Select your plan. I recommend that new bloggers get the basic plan. Click "Select" to choose your plan.**

3. **Type in your domain name in the left box and then click "next" to start the registration process.**

> If you already own a domain name and want to use it for your blog, type your existing domain in the right box and then click "next". Only use the right box if you have previously paid to register a domain!

4. **Fill out your billing details on the registration page.**

5. **You will also need to choose your hosting package and options.**

> All packages have everything you need to get your blog up and running, including a free domain name, easy WordPress blog installation, web hosting, and branded email accounts (e.g. yourname@yourdomain.com).
>
> The 36 month package gets you the lowest monthly rate, while the 12 month package has a lower up-front cost.

I uncheck the boxes next to the other products when I sign-up. You can always get these products later if you decide you need them.

6. You will then need to create a password for your account.

Once you do that you can choose a basic design template for your blog (you can easily change this later, as you will see).

Now your blog software (WordPress) will be installed. Once the install is complete click "Start Building" to be logged-in to your blog.

If the "Start Building" link doesn't work, click "go to my BlueHost account". You will then be able to login to your blog by clicking "Log in to WordPress".

Step 3: Customize Your Blog

Logging in

If you are not already logged-in, go to Bluehost.com and click "Login" on the top right to bring up the login screen. You can then login using your domain name and the password you set in the previous step. If you have misplaced your password you can reset it by clicking the "Forgot Password" link.

Once you log-in you will be taken to your BlueHost Portal. From the portal you can click "Log in to WordPress" to be logged-in automatically to your blog.

Changing your blog design

Once you login you will be in the WordPress administrator area. This is where you can make any changes you want to your blog.

Everyone has a different idea of how they want their blog to look. One of the great things about a WordPress blog is that you can change your entire layout and design with just a few clicks.

In WordPress, blog layouts are known as "Themes". What is a blog theme? Themes control the entire design of your blog. To change your theme you are going to click on the "Appearance" tab on the left menu.

You will see several themes are already installed on your blog: Twenty Seventeen, Twenty Sixteen, etc. These are well-designed, clean-looking themes that can work for just about any type of blog. In fact, many of the world's top bloggers use one of these themes.

Unless you have a very specific design in mind for your blog, I suggest you use one of these themes to start with. For our example, let's use the "Twenty Sixteen" theme. In order to activate the theme on your blog, hover over the theme and click the "Activate" button. That's it! You have changed the entire design of your blog with just one click!

If you don't like any of the themes that are already installed you can easily choose from thousands of other free themes. To install a new theme, click on the "Appearance" tab on the left menu and then click "Add New Theme".

This is the theme search screen. There are thousands of themes to choose from. You can change your entire design at anytime simply by activating a new theme. To find a theme you like, I suggest you click on the "Popular" tab and start browsing. When you find one that you like click the blue "Install" button.

Once the theme is installed click "Activate" to activate the theme on your blog. To see your new theme in action, go to your blog and take a look!

Changing your theme is the simplest way to customize your blog, but there are lots of other customizations you can do.

Step 4: How to Write A Blog Post & Publish It

Now that your blog is up and running it's time to actually do some blogging!

Go to the left menu and click on "Posts".

You will see there is already a post there. This is a default post on every new WordPress blog, and we don't need it. To delete it click "Trash" just under the post.

To begin writing a new post, click the "Add New" link.

You are now on the post editor screen. Enter the title of your post in the top box and then begin writing your post in the lower box.

If you would like to add a picture to your post, click on the "Add Image" icon and click "Upload" to upload a picture from your computer. You can make adjustments to the picture size on the next screen. When you are ready click "Insert into post" to add the picture.

Once you have finished your post just click the "Publish" button on the top right side of the screen to publish it.

Even after you have written a post your blog may still be showing a "Coming Soon" page.

When you are ready to make your blog public just click the "BlueHost" menu at the top left of the menu in your administrator area then click the blue "Launch" button to remove the "Coming Soon" page.

Congratulations! You now know how to start your own blog and publish content!

Step 5: Promote Your Blog

Creating a well-designed blog and writing great content is just the start. In order to get readers for your blog you will need spend some time promoting it, especially when you first start.

Step 6: Make Money Blogging

Once you have put in the effort of creating great blog content and promoting your blog, making money from your blog is actually the easy part.

Blogs have the potential to be extremely lucrative, but don't assume that you're going to start making money in the first week, or even in the first month. It could take six months to a year to start seeing a steady stream of income. Blogging takes work and dedication, but once you develop a large enough audience, there are several methods you can employ to monetize your blog.

How to Promote Your Blog for Free?

How to Promote Your Blog on Other Sites?

1. Comment on other blogs
The right comment on a highly authoritative blog can send you lots of traffic; identify the top blogs in your niche and start interacting and commenting on blogs on a regular basis. This will get the blogger and members of his community to notice you and visit your blog, leading to more traffic for you; you might even get a link, or invitation to guest blog out of it.

2. Develop a blogger outreach plan
Many bloggers fail to get traffic because they take a passive approach to blogging; if you simply publish your article, rest and wait for traffic to come then nothing will happen.

For every article you publish, make sure you have a solid blogger outreach plan; compile a list of dozens of relevant bloggers that you can email your article to and ask them to share or link to your article. This article is a good place to learn how to do blogger outreach.

3. Look for opportunities to be included in link roundups
Every niche has at least a dozen blogs that do weekly or monthly roundups; at the end of the week, or month, these blogs will publish an article with a summary of the most interesting content they read in

a particular month. You can get some nice exposure by emailing these bloggers and asking them to include your article in their next roundup.

4. Enable trackbacks on your blog

Anytime you publish a new article on a blog hosted with WordPress, it gives you an option to enable comments and trackbacks; a "trackback" is an automatic notification sent to any website you link to, allowing your link to be featured in their comments section as well if approved.

If you link to top blogs in your article and you and the blogs you linked to both have trackbacks enabled, a link to your article will appear in their comments section; this will ensure people seeing comments on their blog can see a link to your articles, and it'll eventually lead to more traffic for you.

5. Submit your content to blogging communities

Blogging communities have existed for a long time and are a good place to get traffic; some notable examples are Bizsugar in the business niche, Blokube in the blogging and social media niche and Dribbble in the design niche. Look for a blogging community in your niche that you can share interesting articles with and occasionally submit your articles.

Where to Post Blogs for More Traffic?

1. Guest posts

One of the fastest ways to grow your blog is by writing for other people's blogs; in other words, you can look for a blog that is much bigger than yours and write an article for that blog. You'll be allowed to have a bio that includes a link to your site in your guest post. This can result in a lot of traffic for you.

2. Syndicate your content to top blogs

Many top blogs in your niche will allow you to republish content on their site with credit back to you; most big blogs will do it if they feel that your content is good enough.

Look for a list of publications and network sites in your industry that republish content and see if they'd like to republish your articles.

3. Pursue media syndication opportunities

Many top media sites thrive on publishing a lot of content, and it isn't unusual to see these sites publish 50 or more articles in a single day; of course, this is difficult to pull off and they have to rely on content from guests and other sources to meet their content schedule.

To get around this, top media sites like Lifehacker and Business Insider republish quality content on other sites; often, they only feature content from experts but you can try to reach out to them to see if you can be a part of their content syndication program.

4. Rewrite some of your articles and post them on article directories

Article directories are not as effective as they used to be, but you can rewrite some of your articles in minutes and have them distributed to article directories. Make sure you include links to your blog in these articles.

How to Get People to Read Your Blog More Often?

1. Publish more articles

One of the most effective, but often ignored, blog promotion methods is publishing more articles; research from Hubspot has shown that businesses that publish 16+ blog posts monthly get 3.5 times more traffic and 4.5 times more leads than businesses that publish between 0 – 5 blog posts monthly.

Seven-figure blogger Neil Patel also revealed that his monthly traffic went from 46,134 visitors to 59,787 visitors because he increased content frequency from 1 article to 2 articles weekly.

No matter your niche, research has shown that publishing more content will always lead to an increase in traffic for you; increase your content frequency to 2 or more articles a week, and you'll notice a significant increase in traffic to your blog.

2. Publish longer content

Research has shown that Google and other search engines give preference to longer, comprehensive articles; research by serpIQ that analyzed top 10 results for over 20,000 keywords came to the conclusion that Google ranks content that has more than 2,000 words better than content with fewer words.

Research by Buzzsumo, in a partnership with Moz, which analyzed over 1 million articles, found that articles that are 3,000 – 10,000 words get twice as many shares and 3 times the links that content with fewer than 1,000 words get.

In the Neil Patel article we referenced earlier, he also reveals that one of the top reasons why his blogs get a lot of traffic is because he writes in-depth and comprehensive articles; the average article on Neil's blog ranges from 4,000 to 8,000 words, and the result is that he ranks for lots of long-tail keywords, which leads to significant traffic on the long run.

3. Start an email list

Ask most successful bloggers what the top source of traffic to their blog is and they'll tell you that email is in the top 3. Highly successful blogger Darren Rowse always records a traffic spike (the kind that almost doubles his blog traffic) whenever he sends an email to his list about a new blog post.

Email is such a powerful medium for generating traffic that many bloggers vouch for it; the reason is simple, all things being equal, your email list will only keep growing and rarely decrease. Even more, unlike your blog traffic that can fluctuate, you have access to a database of the people on your email list and can always email them.

The best email management tool is Constant Contact. I recommend you sign up and start building your list immediately. You can get a 20% discount if you purchase here. Don't wait.
If you haven't started building an email list, start now. Install the free SumoMe plugin and use their email list building options including the ScrollBar, Popup and Welcome Mat.

4. Effectively leverage email signatures

Many of us interact with hundreds or even thousands of emails every month; these are some nice eyeballs for your blog, and you can convert them to readers by including a link to your blog in your email signature.

5. Translate your blog posts into other languages

Translating your blog into another language is an effective but little-known way to boost traffic to your blog; this works because translated versions of your blog will start to rank in the country-specific search engines of the languages you translate into. Back when Neil Patel was writing on QuickSprout, he reported a 47% increase in traffic to his blog by translating his blog into 82 languages (screenshot below); translating his blog didn't cost Neil anything as he used the Transposh plugin.

6. Get your blog listed in Google News

Being included in Google news can result in a massive boost in traffic to your blog, especially if you're first to cover major events. If you cover news-related stuff, be sure to apply for inclusion in Google News.

7. Write for the scanner

Research shows that on average, most web users won't read more than 28% of words on a website; in other words, while having longer, comprehensive articles will help your search engine rankings it won't increase the chances of your content being read; the more people read your content, the more people will share it and the more traffic you will get. The solution to this problem is to write your content for scanners.

Using headings and subheadings, bold, italics, numberings, and bullets, you can make your blog content more presentable and scannable, and as a result boost traffic to your blog.

8. Master the best time to post

Research shows that the success of a viral campaign can be influenced by the time that campaign is started as well; a study by BuzzSumo that analyzed over 100 million articles came to the conclusion that the best day to publish an article is on a Tuesday, and that articles published on a Tuesday generally get up to 3X more views than articles published on Sundays.

Find out the best time to post a blog on your site and use this knowledge to effectively promote your content.

How to Get Your Blog Noticed on Social Media?

1. Run a blogging contest
Host your own blogging contest and make it a condition that participants share your article on social media or blog about it; if possible, try to get some sponsors and have them blog about your contest as well. This will go a long way to boost your blog's reach.

2. Develop and execute a social media strategy
Simply creating social media profiles and sharing your latest articles won't cut it. Develop a social media strategy by focusing only on key social networks, engaging with influencers and top pages, and, interacting in groups to grow your social media reach.

Also, make sure you constantly post updates, and regularly recycle old articles on social media; simply sharing your article once, or once in a while, won't cut it. Most popular bloggers share links to old articles on their blog for years. Posting frequency should vary depending on the social media site; research shows that it is optimal to post twice daily on Facebook, thrice daily on Twitter and Google+ and 5 times daily on Pinterest.

3. Feature or interview owners & influencers of popular social media groups
There are several Facebook and LinkedIn groups with thousands and tens of thousands of followers; unfortunately, most people try to get traffic by spamming these social media groups, only to end up having their articles removed.

A better way to get traffic from social media groups is to interview owners, or influencers, of these groups and ask them to share the article you feature them in. Even if they do not share your article, you can share it in the group yourself as a member of the group.

4. Include social share buttons on your blog

Many bloggers fail to include social sharing buttons on their blogs and this is costing these bloggers social shares, exposure, and traffic. While it is not clear to what extent, research shows that adding social share buttons to your page will lead to more shares of your content and as a result increased traffic.

5. Reduce the number of share buttons on your blog

While above we mentioned that including social sharing buttons on your blog can help increase traffic and social shares, there's the paradox of choice factor to consider as well; research shows that giving people too many choices will ensure that they do not make any. In other words, having 10 social sharing buttons on your blog will make sure that your readers use none.

Smashing Magazine also noted that removing Facebook share buttons led to more traffic from Facebook, since readers now directly share their articles on their Facebook timeline instead of liking it (and shares result in more traffic than likes). So that's a consideration for a button you might want to remove.

6. Facebook groups

Facebook groups can also be a good source of traffic and exposure for your blog but, unfortunately, many people fail to get results because they approach these groups in a wrong way and can barely be differentiated from spammers.

In a case study analyzing how he increased traffic from Facebook groups by 3,000%, Bruce Zhang revealed that the best way to get traffic from Facebook groups isn't just to post your links; instead, make sure to use catchy text images as well as a compelling message that shows how people will benefit by reading your article.

7. LinkedIn groups
Similar to Facebook Groups, LinkedIn groups are a good source of traffic. Sharing your content with just your LinkedIn connections won't send you traffic; instead, look for the top LinkedIn groups in your niche, join them and occasionally submit your best articles to them.

8. Promote your blog on Pinterest
Pinterest can be a great source of traffic for your blog and many bloggers have leveraged it with a great source to massively boost their blog traffic; Mandy Wallace was able to take her new blog to 1,000 daily visitors largely thanks to Pinterest. Look for quality interesting images, and focus on using irresistible headlines and you'll be getting quality Pinterest traffic in no time.

9. Leverage sound bites to increase social shares
According to successful blogger and psychology expert, Derek Halpern, "a sound bite is a short message, often no longer than 10 words, that describes the main idea of your content or sales message."

Essentially, a sound bite is a persuasive summary of the message of your article that is easy to remember and easy to quote; because it is short and persuasive, people can, and will, share it, leading to more traffic for you. Mainly due to using this technique, Derek Halpern was able to generate 300 shares and around 9,000 hits for one of his article.

10. Tweetables and shareables

Similar to sound bites, Tweetables and Shareables help you get more traffic by encouraging people to share your content; a "Tweetable" is a message you highlight from your article and design to be shared on Twitter while a "Sharable" can be shared on any social network.

You've probably visited your favorite blogs to see "Click to tweet" embedded inside the article? Well, that's a Tweetable.

Highlight key points all through your article and use sites like Click to Tweet to get people to share your key points. Below is a screenshot that shows a Click to Tweet in one of Michael Hyatt's articles.

11. Leverage "social locker" technology

One of the most creative ways to promote your blog is by restricting part of your content and making people share your article to access it; Will Franco did this by creating an article and adding a "social locker" to his article; the result of this was 11X more shares compared to the average article on his blog.

12. Leverage hashtags when promoting a blog on social media

You can also boost your readership by using #hashtags when promoting your articles on social media; by using relevant hashtags, you'll make your content discoverable when people search for content in your niche, and you'll also benefit should a hashtag you use become trending around the time you used it.

13. Publish regular infographics

Research shows that infographics shared on Twitter get 823% more retweets than images and articles. Neil Patel reveals that infographics have been so effective for him, often helping him catapult his blogs from no traffic to over 100,000 visitors monthly. In his words, old infographics generate more than 50,000 monthly visitors to one of his blogs.

You can promote your blog by creating good looking infographics, especially those that share important facts and statistics and tell influencers in your niche to share it and republish it. You should also submit your infographics to several infographics directories.

14. Retweet old articles

Research shows that only 1.4% (and I suspect that the actual number is much lower) of your Twitter followers will engage with your Tweet; the question is, what happens to the remaining 98.6% of your followers who will not see your Tweet? How do you get their attention? The answer to this is to constantly retweet old blog posts.

Many successful bloggers routinely share old articles, and it isn't unusual to see a blogger sharing the same article 30 – 50 times in the span of a few months; this ensures that people who did not see your content at first will see it later down the line.

Blog Promotion Using Other Media

1. Feature or interview owners of popular forums

Compile a list of the biggest forum owners in your niche and interview them; if possible, get them to participate in a round-up post on your blog. Send them a link after your article has been published and encourage them to share it.

2. Promote your blog on top forums in your niche

Forums can also be a good source of traffic; many of the top forums in your niche probably get millions of monthly visitors, and many have hundreds of thousands of members, but you can't simply start spamming the forums with your links.

Instead, focus on making valuable contributions to the forum in form of ideas, response to other people's discussions and being active in popular discussions; make sure to have a link to your blog in your forum signature, and you'll notice an increase in your traffic.

3. Publish slides to Slideshare

Do you know that Slideshare is popularly known as the sleeping giant of content marketing. The reason for this is simple; over 70 million professionals use Slideshare, and it is one of the 100 most visited websites in the world. The good news is that you can use it to promote your blog.

In a case study, Ana Hoffman revealed that by publishing 9 presentations on Slideshare she was able to generate 243,000 views to her slides and over 1,400 clicks to her blog in 30 days; as a result, Slideshare became her second largest referral traffic. Now, that's one great way to promote a blog!

Create your own Slideshare presentations too, using fewer words and visually rich images to communicate your points, and watch your traffic grow.

4. Look for interview opportunities
There are blogs and websites that are dedicated to interviewing successful people and showcasing their stories; if you have an exciting story or have a success that you can showcase, you can reach out to these websites and ask them to interview you. A good example is IdeaMensch, and there many more similar sites.

5. Promote your blog on Quora
Exactly how powerful is Quora for promoting your blog? As mentioned earlier, Quora superstar Oliver Emberton used Quora to launch a popular blog. Within 7 months of starting his blog, he was already getting millions of views monthly. Oliver did this by contributing great value and being very active on Quora; eventually, this paid off in quality traffic that led to articles on his blog going viral.

6. Ask podcasts to interview you
Similar to being interviewed on sites, you can ask podcast shows to interview you; many podcasters will happily oblige if they find that you have an exciting story.

7. Identify top community and Q&A sites in your niche and participate regularly

Sites like Yahoo! Answers and other niche-specific communities and Q&A sites can be a good source of traffic. Participate in relevant popular discussions and occasionally include a link back to learn more on your blog.

8. Convert your blog posts into PDFs and submit to PDF/document sharing sites

Convert your blog posts into a PDF and submit it to PDF sharing sites; make sure that the final PDF file includes your bio and a link to your site so that people know how to find your blog after they finish reading the PDF.

9. Start a podcast

Data from Edison Research shows that there are more than 46 million podcast listeners in America; podcasts are quickly becoming the best way people consume content because it makes it easy to consume content on a commute while exercising and in a lot of comfortable positions. Boost your blog traffic today by starting your own podcast.

Here's a good case study from someone who created a podcast that was downloaded by over 1,000,000 people.

10. Convert your blog posts into presentations and share on presentation sites

Turn your blog posts into Presentations and submit them to top presentation sites.

11. Submit your blog to blog/website directories

While not as effective as they used to be, blog and website directories can still be a good source of traffic. Being listed in some blog and website directories can also boost traffic to your blog. Here's a list of free website directories you can submit your blog to.

12. Join H.A.R.O.

H.A.R.O, also known as Help A Reporter Out, is a platform that brings reporters and "sources" together; when looking for sources to quote in an article, reporters often visit H.A.R.O to find people to interview. If you have a relevant story that a reporter needs, then you might be mentioned as a source when the reporter publishes their article; just tell the reporter to mention your website in the article if relevant/possible.

13. Create an app for your blog

Create an app for your blog and submit it to Google store and Apple store; regularly invite your readers to download your app and feature it on relevant app sites. If more people download your app, Google will start showcasing it to more of their readers and this will boost your traffic.

14. Convert your blog posts into a podcast and distribute to podcast and audio sites

Research from the Zenspill link above shows that an estimated 33% of Americans have listened to a podcast and that a total of 2.6 billion podcast download requests were made in 2014. Seven-figure blogger Pat Flynn credits his podcast to be one of the top ways new users find his blog.

If you can't start a podcast, you can record an audio version of your blog posts and submit them to podcast sites.

15. Create your own website theme
Create your own website theme with a link back to your website in the footer; there'll be a link to visit your blog on every website that uses your theme. Be sure to make the link nofollow so that it doesn't give you problems with Google and other search engines.

16. Create your own website plugins
Similar to having your own theme, create your own plugins and give people that use it an option to link back to your blog.

17. Leverage image sharing sites to grow your reach
Image sharing sites like Flickr have millions of users, and this presents you with a great opportunity to increase your reach; take cool pictures around you that you own a copyright to, and publish them on these sites with a Creative Commons license on the condition that those who use them must link to you.

This will result in bloggers using your images and linking to you, and occasionally top media sites will use your images and send you some quality traffic.

How to Get Traffic to Your Blog via Collaboration?

1. Create case studies of influencers and ask them to share

Identify influencers in your niche with good reach, do a case study about these influencers and get them to share it. A good example is this case study of Quora influencer Oliver Emberton; Oliver shared the article on social media when it went live which eventually resulted in 100s of shares and thousands of views. The article also ranks on page 1 for his name in Google, bringing in long-term search traffic.

2. Feature other bloggers in your articles and ask them to share

One of the techniques superstar blogger Neil Patel uses to grow his blog is that of linking to dozens of bloggers inside his articles (according to him, his articles usually contain 100+ links) and then reaching out to the bloggers who he linked to letting them know that he linked to them. The result is hundreds, sometimes thousands, of shares per article and eventually lots of traffic back to him.

Regularly link to other bloggers in your articles and email all of them to let them know about your article; many of them will share your article, resulting in lots of traffic for you.

3. Do "expert roundups" and ask featured experts to share

How will you like to leverage the reach of 10, 20 or more experts in your niche to grow yours? Is this even possible? Yes, by doing "expert roundups" in which you interview a group of experts and ask them one or two questions to be compiled inside one article, you can massively boost your blog traffic.

Once your expert roundup has been published, ask all the bloggers featured to spread the word about it; the result of this will often be thousands of extra visitors to your blog.

A good example of an expert roundup is this article that features 32 bloggers who reveal their favorite site-building platform; the result is hundreds of shares.

4. Join communities where bloggers support each other (or exchange shares)

There are secret bloggers club and websites that foster a community where members promote themselves; in short, every community member promotes each other's content and benefit from the support of a massive community. Two good examples are JustRetweet and Triberr.

5. Do cross-promotion with other bloggers

Find a blogger with a similar audience to yours and see if you can do a "shout out exchange"; in other words, you mention them on your blog and they mention you on theirs. You can also promote them to your email list while they promote you to theirs.

6. Be an influential blogger's success story

While most bloggers struggle to get traffic, authority bloggers with hundreds of thousands of readers go over and beyond to send traffic to people who can validate them; if you take the advice of a popular blogger and get results from it, he will happily showcase you to his audience and send traffic back to you.

How to Get Blog Traffic via Search Engines?

1. Optimize your blog for search engines

Search engines are the #1 source of traffic for most established blogs.

The above screenshot shows traffic to an authority blog in one month; you can see that out of 582,000 visitors, 476,000 came from search engines. That's how powerful search traffic is; after all, Google is the biggest website in the world!

Many bloggers ignore basic SEO, and they eventually suffer from it. Most successful bloggers get as much as 50% or more of their traffic from search engines; taking the right measures when it comes to SEO can double your blog traffic within a short period of time.

Things like using the right title tags, having a catchy description, ensuring that your site is easy to navigate, etc, can lead to a significant increase in traffic to your blog.

It's important that you don't ignore SEO techniques; familiarize yourself with the concept of SEO and optimize your blog and your articles to rank well for relevant keywords in Google and other search engines.

2. Make your website faster

Research shows that a one second delay in website loading time will result in a 7 percent loss in conversion, and that slow websites cost the U.S. e-commerce market $500 billion annually.

Not just this, but you'll also lose 40 percent of visitors to your website if it takes longer than 3 seconds to load. If your website is slow, then you're already losing half your visitors. Make your website faster and watch your traffic increase significantly.

3. Constantly refresh old posts

One of Google's ranking factors is content freshness, and this reportedly affects as much as 35% of Google searches; this supports research from Hubspot that shows that blogs that publish 16+ articles monthly get 3.5X more traffic than blogs that publish less than 4 articles monthly.

One way to benefit from Google's freshness algorithm is by publishing more articles on your blog, while another way is by updating old articles; review articles you published months and years ago, eliminate outdated information and bring them forward. This will impact your blog's search rankings and lead to more traffic.

4. Proper SEO slug/permalink structure

Do you know that your blog's SEO slug/permalink structure can go a long way to influence your search rankings and traffic to your blog? The best SEO slug is the one that includes your title in a descriptive way while removing unnecessary words like verbs.

5. Proper site structure

Just as a good SEO slug is important, it's also important to have a proper site structure; make sure your site structure makes it easy for search engines to index your content. Make sure that every page on your blog is indexable, and have an archives page or sitemap that will make it easy for search engines to crawl your content.

This Neil Patel article shares practical tips to help you create a site structure that will enhance your blog's SEO.

6. Deep internal links

Internal links are an essential part of your on-page SEO, and quality internal links will impact your rankings in the search engines. Make sure you regularly link to relevant pages and articles on your blog.

7. Have a keyword research strategy

Many bloggers have lackluster search rankings and, as a result, poor search traffic due to not having a keyword research strategy; do you utilize any of the best keyword research tools before publishing an article on your blog, or do you just publish new articles?

Incorporating a keyword research strategy into your content marketing strategy will go a long way to boost traffic to your blog.

8. Focus on the mobile experience

Research shows that the number of mobile internet users has now exceeded the number of desktop internet users. Google also recently made an upgrade to their algorithm that favored sites that were optimized for mobile users and that penalized sites that were not optimized for mobile users.

Some sites lost as much as 46.6% of their search traffic due to not having a mobile-optimized site while some gained as much as 30.1% traffic by having a mobile-friendly website.

Something as simple as optimizing your blog for mobile users can give you a traffic boost, so make sure you have a website that is focused on a better mobile experience for your readers.

9. Link to a lot of authoritative sources

Google uses a lot of factors to rank websites, including how many links point to a website, but very few people know that Google also ranks you based on how many people you link to.

If your website constantly links to authoritative websites and resources that are relevant to your niche, Google will assume that you're a good and authoritative resource in your niche, and they'll rank you better as a result; this, in turn, will lead to more traffic for you.

How to Promote A Blog Using Content Marketing?

1. Publish a resource article

Resource articles are exceptionally effective for boosting traffic to your blog, much more than the average blog post; this article on Digital Current shows that it's possible to get 100,000 views per article by publishing resource articles, and that resource articles can get up to 10,000% more views than the average article.

2. Create an ultimate/advanced guide

An ultimate guide is designed to be the first and last article your readers read on a subject; due to their nature, ultimate guides are usually very comprehensive in nature. It isn't unusual to see an ultimate guide that is 5,000 – 10,000 words.

As we saw earlier in this article, search engines favor comprehensive articles rank them better; people love them too, so they'll share them massively. By publishing an ultimate guide, you'll benefit from all angles.

Once you've published your ultimate guide, reach out to bloggers in your niche and ask them to spread the word about it.

3. Write controversial posts

Writing controversial posts, or attacking sacred cows in your niche, can be very powerful for generating traffic and boosting your exposure. If you Google it, there are many stories about how publishing a controversial post can help skyrocket a blogger's fame and traffic.

4. Blog about a major personality

So what does blogging about Obama, or Justin Beiber or some other major personality have to do with promoting your blog? In June 2010, Think Traffic published an article titled "The Diddy Guide to Constant Creativity and Relentless Marketing"; the result was a Tweet of the article by P. Diddy himself to his 2.6 million Twitter followers.

5. Publish your own 101 list

Earlier on we examined research that shows that Google favors articles that are above 2,000 words. Top lists of 101 items are usually very in-depth and comprehensive, and as a result they generate a lot of traffic; the fact that list posts get a lot of shares and traffic is backed up by data, and the Buzzsumo/Moz study that we referenced earlier shows that List posts get significantly more shares and links than other types of content.

6. Publish an ultimate link/list roundup

Compile and publish an ultimate list of resources/articles on a particular topic; include as many relevant resources as possible and email all the bloggers you featured on your list and ask them to share your article.

7. Key into major events

A major election, death, birth, sports event, etc? Smart bloggers are creative, and as a result, they know how to leverage happenings around them to boost their reach and influence.

When major events happen, lots of people tend to get interested and start searching for it on search engines and social media; by capitalizing on this and using an angle relevant to your niche, you can get quality traffic. Example: "What the Superbowl Can Teach Us About Successful Blogging" or "What the Election Debates Can Teach You About Success", etc. You get the idea? No matter the event, you can tie it to your blog's topic and capitalize on it to boost traffic.

8. Improve your headlines

Do you know that a simple headline change can result in a massive boost in traffic to your blog? According to Copyblogger, on average, 8 out of 10 people will read your headline but only 2 out of 10 will read your content. This is why it is very important to learn how to write better headlines and put serious effort into your headlines.

A case study that demonstrates how much of a difference the right headline can make was featured on Lifehacker; a New York Times article was originally titled "How Companies Learn Your Secrets" and it only managed to get 12,902 views. The very same article was republished on Forbes and retitled "How Target Figured out a Teen Girl Was Pregnant Before Her Father Did" and got a whopping 680,000 views. That's over 600,000 more views than the original articles, and that's interesting considering that The New York Times is a much bigger site than Forbes. The difference in traffic was solely due to the headline.

In revealing why their articles go viral, Upworthy revealed that they write at least 25 headlines for every post they publish, they test the best ones and go with the very best one; if Upworthy, a site that gets over 87 million visitors monthly, does this, you have no reason not to.

9. Publish a controversial response to top bloggers or thought leaders

When an industry leader publishes an article or says something that you disagree with; publish a response on your blog explaining why you disagree with the industry leader. Most industry leaders will share your article, especially if your response is well-thought-out and informative.

Promote Your Blog Using Other Peoples Content

1. Invite others to guest post on your blog

Guest blogging on other blogs is indeed a powerful way to get traffic and gain exposure to your blog, but inviting others to guest post for your own blog can be equally powerful.

If you invite others to write for you, especially if they have a much bigger reach than you do, they are more likely to share their guest post with their readers. The result of this will be more traffic to your blog.

2. Start paying people to write for you

There are websites that regularly publish lists of sites that pay writers, and these lists occasionally get tens of thousands of views and hundreds of links thus making them highly authoritative. By offering to pay people to write articles on your blog, and emailing the publishers of these lists to include your website, you'll be getting an instant boost in traffic and an authoritative backlink.

3. Offer incentives to people writing for you

A technique that can give you a massive boost in traffic to your blog is incentivizing contributions to your blog; whether you pay writers for articles or accept guest posts, you'll be able to get more traffic by compensating people whose articles become your most popular post or get a certain number of views in a month.

4. Leverage user-generated content

Forums, comments and other types of user-generated content can be big wins for your blog; Mizzou Alumni Association was able to boost their site traffic by 15% while Chobani experienced a 225.9%

increase in revenue by leveraging the power of User Generated Content.

5. Ask experts to contribute advice to your article

One very effective way to unleash an avalanche of traffic on your blog is by asking experts to contribute their advice to your articles; this is especially effective if you've written an ultimate guide to a subject or a long list of articles with a lot of points. Identify key experts in your niche for various points and ask them to give you their input; include their input inside your article and let them know when it goes live so that they can share. This technique is highly underutilized, but it's so powerful that Jimmy Daly of GetVero was able to get 36,282 people to read a single article on his blog.

6. Email people with lists of blogs that accept guest posts

There are hundreds of lists of different blogs that accept guest posts online, and many of these lists are read by thousands of people weekly; if you accept guest posts on your blog, email these bloggers and ask them to include your blog on their list. This won't just result in some nice traffic and potentially quality contributions to your blog, but it will also yield an authoritative backlink that can help your search traffic.

How to Advertise Your Blog?

1. Advertise on Reddit

Reddit is one of the biggest online communities, with an estimated 17 million monthly users. While many people are familiar with advertising on Facebook, Google Adwords and other PPC options, very few people pay attention to Reddit; surprisingly, Reddit's CPM, at $0.75 CPM, is much lower compared to bunch of other social media sites.

2. Advertise on Facebook

Facebook is increasingly becoming most brand's favorite advertising platform, and rightfully so. Facebook has in-depth understanding of your audience and allows you to target your content to them; also, advertising on Facebook is 3 times cheaper than Google Ads.

3. Advertise on AdWords

Sign up for an AdWords account and sit back and wait for Google to send you a free trial offer. Happens quite a lot!

4. Do solo ads

A "solo ad" is an email newsletter that only contains an ad; so if someone emails their list and a recommendation of your blog or product is the only thing in that email, that's a solo ad. Solo ads can be great for boosting blog traffic; find relevant bloggers in your niche with good email lists and offer them a fee in exchange for sending an ad to their list about your blog/email list.

Promote Your Blog Using Freebies and Competitions

1. Sponsor a blogging contest

Blogging contests are being run every day, and sponsoring one can result in some nice traffic and quality backlinks for you; most contests will make it a requirement to blog about the contest and link to the website of their sponsors and this is where you benefit. Look for blogging contests of this nature and see how you can participate.

2. Run a viral giveaway

Viral giveaways can have a massive impact on your bottom line, and a good case study to this effect is Josh Earl, who was able to get 482,044 people to visit his blog and 187,991 people to subscribe to his blog in just 11 days. Now, that's a phenomenal result!

If you're struggling to get traffic to your blog, perhaps it's time to start your own viral giveaway; look for a product that is in high demand in your niche and offer people an opportunity to win it by joining your giveaway. Let their chances of winning increase by inviting more people to join your giveaway.

3. Create a free viral report ebook

Create a high-value, concise ebook and make it available for free, no strings attached (don't even ask for an email). Now, share that ebook everywhere you can and encourage readers to share it as well, be sure to include a bio inside the ebook. Corbett Barr did this in 2010 with his ebook "18 Months, 2 Blogs, Six Figures". The result was that this ebook led to a massive increase in traffic to his blog, and lots of new subscribers.

4. Run a blogging challenge

In 2013, Natalie Sisson was about to do a book launch and decided to run a blogging challenge; the challenge was a 30 Day Blog Challenge designed to coincide with the launch of her book, and she reports it to be the most successful initiative she's ever run on her blog.

The blogging challenge led to a 100% increase in traffic, 1,000 new subscribers to her list and her book becoming a #1 bestseller the week it was published.

Blogging challenges can unite your community and make them passionately involved in your project, and this will always lead to more traffic to your blog.

5. Run a traffic contest

Invite members of your community to promote your blog and do their best to send traffic to your blog for a whole month, award the people who send the most traffic a prize.

6. Give viral list building a shot

Prepare a series of incentives and design a viral list building system; start with a basic incentive that will be your opt in incentive, then offer people more attractive incentives if they share your content or invite a number of people to join your list.

How to Promote Your Blog Using Your Products?

1. Join bundle offers to expand your reach

Occasionally, there are events such as Only72 that offer a bundle of products for a limited period of time at a discount price; the time limit and discount is the appeal of this, and it isn't unusual to see hundreds of thousands of people hearing about the offer and thousands of people taking advantage of it.

If you have a product, reach out to organizers of these events and ask them to include your product; you'll be increasing your reach due to the cross-promotion other, often more influential, participants and affiliates will do.

2. Give affiliates 100% commission on your products

If you have a product, it's much easier to get traffic to your blog. Identify influencers with a big blog and email list, especially if they have no product, and offer them 100% commissions for every sale of your products that they make. Make sure you get all buyers of your product to subscribe to your email list, and you win; you win because those buyers might not otherwise know about you, but now they are readers who have bought a product you created.

3. Sell your products on promo sites at a massive discount

While it might not look like a win to sell your products on sites that offer products at a massive discount, it can be a big win if this suddenly exposes you to thousands of new people; find sites of this nature and offer your product at a discount. Make sure people are required to sign up to your email list before they can access your product.

4. Leverage kindle free promotions to boost your reach

If you sell an ebook, you can also leverage limited-time Kindle promotions to boost your email list; Tristan King was able to get 600% more people to download his ebook by leveraging Kindle's KDP ebook promotion system, and that gave him a nice boost in readership.

Other Ways to Get Free Blog Traffic

1. Organize events in your area and tell attendees to visit your blog

Organize offline education events in your area in partnership with schools, churches, and communities. Make your events entertaining and educative, and invite attendees to read your blog.

2. Take advantage of local media

The online and blogging craze is so high that many people now fail to realize the power of offline media. Seek out radio presenters, TV presenters, local magazines and newspapers in your country and ask them if they want an expert in your capacity. Due to the blogging craze, fewer people are disturbing them than used to be; this increases your chances of actually getting coverage, resulting in a boost in your brand image and blog traffic.

3. Include elements of transparency

If done right, transparency can be a very powerful weapon for promoting your blog. Several top blogs and startups can testify to this; seven-figure blogger Pat Flynn is a good example; one of the techniques he used to accelerate his blog growth was publishing income reports.

People were excited about his income reports, so they visited it en mass and shared it a lot; it is also widely linked to across the web. Startups like Buffer and Groove are also using this principle to grow their blogs and business; by being transparent, they get people excited about what they are doing and this leads to more exposure for them.

4. Publish a list of power users in your industry or on a social media site

Many of these power users will get an ego boost from this and will share your content on social media.

5. Listen to your readers

Sometimes, you'll notice that certain articles on your blog will become big hits while some will barely get read by anybody; oftentimes, the reason for this has to do with demand for the topic an article covers. If an article is in high demand, it'll do a great job of promoting itself and traffic will only keep increasing; if an article has low demand, the promotion you do will yield minimal results.

Ask your readers what content they want to read about the most, and create your content based on popular demand.

6. Analyze your blog traffic

The key to blogging success lies in identifying what's working and doing more of it; once your blog starts to gain traction and get some readership, start paying special attention to your blog traffic to see what kind of content is getting the most views. If you notice a trend with a certain type of content, do more of that type of content and you can be assured of increased traffic.

7. Only offer partial blog feed, or customize your feed

If you own a blog, you're most probably allowing people to consume your blog content through feed readers; a great way to capitalize on this to boost blog traffic is either by offering partial feeds, or by customizing your feeds in such a way that you can include a note and link to your blog/article below the feed. The benefit of doing this is two-fold:

- It gets readers to come directly to your blog; this increases the likelihood of them sharing your article, thereby leading to more traffic for you.
- It ensures that you get attribution when your content is being scraped; a lot of sites scrape content via feeds without attribution, and this isn't good if there's no way for you to get credit back to your blog.

8. Use images in all your blog posts

Research shows that articles with images get 94% more views compared to articles without images. Make sure every article on your blog include one or more relevant and appealing image, and this will significantly boost traffic to your blog.

9. Create an industry survey and make the results public

Invite your readers to answer a survey about topics of major interest to your niche, publish your survey results and create an infographic about it. Email bloggers in your niche to notify them about your survey results and ask them to write about it.

How to Make Money with Your Blog?

1. Monetize with CPC or CPM Ads

One of the most common ways bloggers make money is through placing ads on their site. There are two popular types of ads:

- **CPC/PPC Ads:** Cost per click (also called pay per click) ads are usually banners that you place in your content or sidebar. Each time a reader clicks on the ad, you are paid for that click.
- **CPM Ads:** CPM Ads, or "cost per 1,000 impressions," are ads that pay you a fixed amount of money based on how many people view your ad.

Perhaps the most popular network for placing these types of ads is Google AdSense. With this program, you do not need to be in direct contact with advertisers; you simply place the banner on your site, Google chooses ads relevant to your content, and your viewers click on the ads. There are countless similar programs available if you find that AdSense doesn't work for you, such as Chitika, Infolinks, and Media.net.

2. Sell Private Ads

Working with advertising networks isn't your only option when it comes to selling ads. If you end up with enough traffic, advertisers may come directly to you and ask you to place their ad on your site. You can also contact advertisers yourself. The biggest difference from the above mentioned option is that there is no middle man, which means you can set your own ad rates.

Selling private ads can come in the form of banners, buttons, or links. You can even make money writing sponsored posts where you write about or give a review of an advertiser's product or service. Another option is to write an underwritten post or series, which is where you can write about any topic, but the advertiser pays for a "Brought to you by" mention in the content.

The ways you make money with this can vary. For instance, you might charge a one-time fee for a link within a post. If you are hosting banner ads, you might charge your partner monthly.

Bonus tip: To maximize your income, you can also choose to sell sponsorship space in your email newsletters, podcasts, and videos.

3. Include Affiliate Links in Your Content

Affiliate marketing is also another great tool for monetizing your blog. Here is how affiliate marketing works:

1. An advertiser has a product she wants to sell. She agrees to give you a commission from each sale if the buyer is coming from your site.
2. She gives you a unique link that tracks your affiliate code. That way, she knows when a buyer used your link to make a purchase.
3. You include your affiliate link on your site. You can do this directly in the content or through banner ads. If a reader clicks on your unique link and buys the product you have recommended, you earn a percentage of what she purchased.

You can utilize affiliate marketing through ad networks like Amazon Associates, or you can create private partnerships with advertisers and businesses with an affiliate program.

4. Sell Digital Products

If you would rather not advertise other people's products on your site, or if you are looking for another stream of income, consider selling digital products. This can include items like:

- eBooks
- Online courses/workshops
- Images, video, or music people can use in their own content
- Apps, plugins, or themes

Just remember that if you are going to choose one of these avenues that you make it relevant and useful to your readers. A lot of bloggers make the mistake of assuming they are developing a product their readers need; listen to your readers first, and then create a digital product that will meet their needs.

5. Use It As A Content Marketing Tool for Your Business

It is also possible to sell physical products on your blog and to make money that way. Instead of thinking of it as making money from your blog, however, think of your blog as a content marketing tool that will drive visitors to your business website.

The possibilities are practically endless when it comes to developing a business blog. You could sell hand-made products, books, manufactured products, and so much more. Or you might already have a business and decide to start a blog to convert loyal customers.

Lets say, for example, that you refurbish and resell used smartphones out of your home. You could use a blog to attract visitors to your website where you list your current phones for sale. Your blog might cover topics about DIY refurbishing. On one level, it seems counterintuitive because you want people to buy your phones, but it also helps you build a brand and gain recognition. Social media guru Jay Baer explains the concept on Copyblogger:

I was at a conference a few years ago, and this is where I first sort of started thinking about this concept, and their founder, Robert Johnson, was speaking…

He said, "Well our best customers are the people that think they can fix it themselves."

But eventually you are going to get out of your depth either on that project on a project down the road, at which point who are you going to call? Are you going to call somebody randomly that you discovered on Google or are you going to call the guys who you just watched their logo in the corner of a 14-minute instructional video?

This concept can also be applied to services in all types of industries. For instance, if you offered electronic repair services as opposed to physical products, you could still use the same blogging concept to increase brand awareness and convert more clients.

6. Sell Memberships

Another option to make money is to sell memberships to exclusive corners of your website. For instance, a career blog might charge $10 per month for users to gain access to their job board. A startup business blog might sell memberships to their forums where people can get personalized advice about their business.

The key here is that your exclusive membership has to be more valuable than something your visitors can find for free somewhere else, so be sure you're developing something of value and worth the price.

7. Use It to Build Your Credibility

Blogging to build credibility can lead to many money-making opportunities. For instance, let us say you start a blog in the finance industry. People start reading your content, and your blog becomes very popular. You are now a recognized figure in the finance industry.

Once you have that authority, people might approach you to co-author a book on debt management, or you could charge to speak at conferences or to run employee financial training days.

This certainly isn't a direct form of making money blogging, but it has worked for many well-known bloggers, and it can work for you, too. If you're looking for a direct revenue stream, popular blogs have sold for 4-7 figures (sometimes more) by selling their branding and content.

The biggest thing to keep in mind is that making money blogging is not possible by putting your site up and letting it sit there. The "if you build it, they will come" mentality doesn't work here, so be sure you're willing to put in the time. Most bloggers don't see a spike of income for several months (sometimes years) after starting their blog.

Before you dive too deep into blogging, remember these little bits of advice:

Create Quality Content

You are not going to make any money from your blog if people don't read it. After all, your readers are the ones who are going to make you money, whether they're clicking on your ads or buying your products. Always put your readers first.

Don't Spend Your Time Exclusively on Your Blog

Developing a successful blog has a lot to do with building relationships. That can include relationships with sponsors, affiliate partners, or simply other bloggers who will direct traffic to your blog. Be sure some of your time is spent on forums and other blogs (or whatever works for you) to build these relationships and your blog.

Don't Be Afraid to Experiment

Not all of these tips and avenues of income are going to work for you. Don't be afraid to tweak your methods to see what works best for you and your readers.

Making money blogging can take a lot of persistence, but it can pay off in the long-run if you're starting out from scratch. Just remember that you don't have to use all of these money-making avenues at once. Consider what other people in your industry are doing, and start from there.

Over time, you will learn what works for you and what doesn't. If you're looking to make money from your blog, which option will you start with?

How To Write Online For Money

How To Write Online For Money

www.ingramcontent.com/pod-product-compliance
Lightning Source LLC
Chambersburg PA
CBHW030505220526
45464CB00006B/2671